Leader

ˈlē'dər

*A 30-Day Devotional on
Biblical Principles for
Modern Leadership Challenges*

ALEX SEZER JR.

HIGH BRIDGE BOOKS
HOUSTON

Leader
by Alex Sezer Jr.

Copyright © 2023 by Alex Sezer Jr.

All rights reserved.

Printed in the United States of America
ISBN (Paperback): 978-1-954943-82-7
ISBN (Hardcover): 978-1-954943-83-4

All rights reserved. Except in the case of brief quotations embodied in critical articles and reviews, no portion of this book may be reproduced, stored in a retrieval system, or transmitted in any form or by any means—electronic, mechanical, photocopy, recording, scanning, or other—without prior written permission from the author.

Scripture quotations marked NIV are taken from THE HOLY BIBLE, NEW INTERNATIONAL VERSION®, NIV® Copyright © 1973, 1978, 1984, 2011 by Biblica, Inc.® Used by permission. All rights reserved worldwide.

Scripture quotations marked ESV are taken from The ESV® Bible (The Holy Bible, English Standard Version®). ESV® Text Edition: 2016. Copyright © 2001 by Crossway, a publishing ministry of Good News Publishers. The ESV® text has been reproduced in cooperation with and by permission of Good News Publishers. Unauthorized reproduction of this publication is prohibited. All rights reserved.

Scripture quotations marked KJV are taken from the King James Version.

High Bridge Books titles may be purchased in bulk for educational, business, fundraising, or sales promotional use. For information, please contact High Bridge Books via www.HighBridgeBooks.com/contact.

Published in Houston, Texas by High Bridge Books.

To Aubree, my little leader, you have bestowed upon me another dimension of leadership. It is my honor to be your dad.

You have all my love.

Contents

Introduction — 1

Day 1: Delegate — 3
Day 2: Calling — 7
Day 3: Vision — 11
Day 4: Price — 15
Day 5: Service — 19
Day 6: Skill — 23
Day 7: Posture — 27
Day 8: Trust — 31
Day 9: Empower — 35
Day 10: Resourceful — 39
Day 11: Responsibility — 43
Day 12: Action — 47
Day 13: Humility — 51
Day 14: Depend — 55
Day 15: Focus — 59
Day 16: Tenacious — 63
Day 17: Gratitude — 67
Day 18: Brand — 71
Day 19: Profit — 75
Day 20: Rooted — 79

Day 21: Promotion _____ 83

Day 22: Secure _____ 87

Day 23: Evaluate _____ 91

Day 24: Authentic _____ 95

Day 25: Treasure _____ 99

Day 26: Attitude _____ 103

Day 27: Proactive _____ 107

Day 28: Patience _____ 111

Day 29: Adapt _____ 115

Day 30: Purpose _____ 119

Introduction

Drawing from my experiences leading the Texas A&M football team as captain, ascending to the presidency of multiple organizations at a young age, and overseeing assets surpassing $75 million with a resident community exceeding 2,000, I have come to understand the paramount importance of effective leadership. I believe that an organization's success hinges on the capabilities of its leaders. My faith has been paramount in guiding me towards leadership success, and that is exactly why I'm sharing what I've learned with you.

This devotional is designed to help Christians move beyond Sunday morning inspiration to Monday morning implementation through a series of thought-provoking devotionals that offer practical points of application. Many Christians struggle to apply the Gospel truth in all facets of their lives, but the Christian lifestyle should not end when we leave the church building. In fact, our Sunday morning church experience should be the beginning of our Christian journeys.

As followers of Christ, we are commanded to be a light to the world, not to keep our faith hidden. We should be leaders in every aspect of industry and life. As cliché as it may sound, we may be the only Jesus some people see. This devotional uses biblical truths and personal stories to demonstrate the power of scripture and its relevance in our lives, particularly in leadership roles. It highlights powerful truths that, when applied, will lead to great success in life. I am confident in this promise.

While I hope that the words of Christ take root in your life and bear fruit, if you only gain personal success, you will have missed the greater purpose. I pray that those around you will see your good works and glorify your Father in heaven. This is not about elevating your name but bringing glory to His name. This devotional is about infiltrating the world with the culture and heartbeat of Christ. I hope it serves as a catalyst for your success and that you bring honor to Christ through your life.

Notes on Structure

Each devotional uses a formulaic approach containing four sections that will take you on a journey from knowing to doing.

1. Information: Each devotional includes a scriptural text and a short story that illustrates the text further. This section informs you as the title implies.
2. Application: What good is information without application? The goal is not solely for you to know the truth but to live it, so I've included practical points of application.
3. Supplication: At the end of every application, you will find a prayer. Prayer is our gateway to God's ears. Whom better to talk to than the God who spoke the world into existence?
4. Implementation: Lastly, there will be a section for you to journal how you plan to implement each lesson in your life. Journaling will help the topic stick and cause you to think deeper about the lesson. This is where transformation happens—when we act on what we know.

Day 1

Delegate

/**del**-i-geyt/
v. to entrust responsibility to another

Information

> *Moses' father-in-law replied, "What you are doing is not good. You and these people who come to you will only wear yourselves out. The work is too heavy for you; you cannot handle it alone."*
>
> —Exodus 18:17–18 NIV

"Who believes? We believe! Who believes? We believe!" I responded with my little league football teammates to our coach's question as intensely as hall-of-fame linebacker Ray Lewis would have before we stormed out of the tunnel to take the field for the championship game. Before kickoff, my coach discreetly ushered me to the side and whispered words that would become the mantra of my life. He said, "Alex, you are the only one who can win this game for us."

Labeled as a go-getter, I've lived life with the weight of the world on my shoulders trying to do everything alone, that is, until I learned about the advice Jethro gave to Moses.

In Exodus 18, we find that Jethro—perhaps on a Bring Your Dad to Work Day—observed his son-in-law Moses and quickly discovered that Moses' operating system was a formula for failure. Moses, the only recognized judge for the large and expanding nation of Israel, was exhausted while hearing cases from dawn till dusk. Trying to do it all alone, Moses spent his most valuable hours frustrated.

Have you ever felt this way? Have you ever found yourself with more work than hours? If so, Jethro's timeless advice on delegation is for you. Jethro not only instructed Moses to have a team, but he gave him specific advice on how to create that team, because not all help is equal. Jethro told Moses to first find people of high character and competency and then delegate authority based on the load each leader could handle. Here is what you should look for as you aim to scale your operation and advance the work of the kingdom.

Application

1. Find capable people: The temptation of Christians in business is to hire people just because of their faith. However, Moses was told to find capable people. You should seek competent help who have the skills necessary to perform their duties with excellence.

2. Never compromise on character: Never, I repeat, never, overlook character flaws because someone is talented. Jethro told Moses to select men who were trustworthy and God-fearing. For our operations to be God-glorifying, the people must be God-fearing. In the same way that we shouldn't hire people solely for their true faith, we cannot hire others for their talent alone.

3. Appoint based on capacity: Entrust people with the level of responsibility they can handle and promote them once they have proven they are capable of more. Not everyone can handle the same load, as evidenced by the varying numbers assigned to each leader Moses appointed.

Supplication

Father, help me to strategically release the things I am not meant to carry alone. I pray that you give me the wisdom to teach and choose partners who bring glory to your name. Amen.

Implementation

Are there areas in your life or work where you need to seek competent help? If so, how can you strategically release the things you are not meant to carry alone?

_____

_____

_____

_____

_____

_____

_____

Day 2

Calling

/kaw-ling/
n. a strong inner impulse toward a course of action especially when accompanied by conviction of divine influence

Information

> *So the Twelve gathered all the disciples together and said, "It would not be right for us to neglect the ministry of the word of God to wait on tables. Brothers and sisters, choose seven men from among you who are known to be full of the Spirit and wisdom. We'll turn this responsibility over to them and will give our attention to prayer and the ministry of the word."*
>
> —Acts 6:2–4 NIV

I unlocked the door and quickly plopped my lifeless body onto the couch. Staring blankly into space, I wondered if my goal of financial freedom was a carrot on a stick illusion to keep me going. After all, I did not feel free ... not even a little bit while doing everything in my business solo. My phone ringer remained on loud indefinitely to alert me of the next problem I needed to solve, and I hadn't had a day off in months. Holding responsibility close to my chest like a mother does a newborn, I began to air out my frustration to my wife. During my pity party, she spoke words of wisdom that hit me in the face like a wet towel. She said, "Just because you are capable of it doesn't mean you're called to it." Torn between shouting, "That'll preach" and "Mind your business," I knew she was right.

Leadership does not mean that you are everything to everyone; it is closer to the opposite. Leaders know how to distinguish between noise and the necessary. I admire the discipline of the disciples in Acts 6 when confronted with the noise from the crowd. There were Christians upset about their widows being overlooked in the lunch line. I imagine it was tempting for the disciples to step in and personally solve the issue. However, the disciples recognized that the problem required their mental capacity to make a strategic decision, not their physical efforts to solve the problem. Waiting tables was not the highest and best use of their time.

Here are some practical steps you can apply to your life to ensure you are using your time properly and in the most edifying way.

Application

1. Discipline your focus: Set your lens on the necessary things. What is the God-given calling on your life that only you can fulfill? Do that.
2. Design your day: Take control over your schedule, proactively setting aside quiet time when you are not responding to daily chaos.
3. Delegate the noise: Your noise is someone else's necessary. Find people who are called to perform the duties that are distractions for you.

Supplication

Father, as I embark on today's journey, help me to recognize the things in my life that are noise, distracting from the necessary. Help me to honor you with disciplined focus, acknowledging that everything I'm capable of completing is not synonymous with all I am called to accomplish. Amen.

Implementation

Reflect on your daily duties and consider—what adjustments can you make to your schedule to better align your tasks to your God-given calling?

_____

_____

_____

_____

_____

_____

_____

Day 3

Vision

/*vizh-uhn*/
n. a thought, concept, or object formed by the imagination

Information

And the Lord answered me: "Write the vision; make it plain on tablets, so he may run who reads it."

—Habakkuk 2:2 ESV

"Siri, what's the best vision statement for a real estate company?" Becoming the president of a company at the ripe age of 24 and being tasked with articulating vision led me to exhaust all lifelines. I was expected to put words to something that had been trapped inside of our founder's head for 30 years and only expressed through his personality. I googled, phoned a friend, and read many books, but none of those things provided clarity. It was not until I turned to God, looked within the organization, and shut off external noise that I found a clear, compelling vision.

Habakkuk faced a similar challenge when tasked to articulate to others the things that God had revealed to him. It was a formidable task to transcribe the vision clearly so that it would remain impactful to both

Habakkuk and all who would read it. God, being omniscient, recognized this challenge and instructed Habakkuk to "make it plain."

So many times, we fall into the temptation of making a vision statement complex instead of compelling. The purpose of a vision statement is not to demonstrate the vast intellect of the writer but to create progress in the life of the reader. Here's how you can accomplish that.

Application

1. Keep it simple: Avoid complexity and strive for clarity. Your team will appreciate the coherence that leads to focus instead of complexity leading to confusion. Practicality and understanding are key ingredients of a well-written vision.
2. Avoid cliches: Vision comes from God, not Google. An authentic vision that comes from within your organization carries more power than a plagiarized vision from Siri. What is God speaking to and through your organization?
3. Reading leads to running: Vision should always lead to action. You know you have created inspiration and trust when your team reads your vision statement and runs towards the company's goals.

Supplication

Father, as you give me a vision on the inside, help me articulate that vision to others, being clear in purpose so that we may all progress. Amen.

Implementation

Think about the relationship between vision and action. What can you do to make sure that your vision statement is clear and inspires your team to make progress towards achieving the organization's goals?

_____
_____
_____
_____
_____
_____
_____

Day 4

Price

/prahys/
n. the cost at which something is obtained

Information

Suppose one of you wants to build a tower. Won't you first sit down and estimate the cost to see if you have enough money to complete it? For if you lay the foundation and are not able to finish it, everyone who sees it will ridicule you, saying, 'This person began to build and wasn't able to finish.'"

—Luke 14:28–30 NIV

"Alex, which one looks the best?" My wife, who is a professional Target shopper loves to question me about fashion and design after she has narrowed her choices down. Unfortunately, my answer is normally wrong and leaves me wondering why she continues to ask for my input. Although wrong, I will give myself some credit for my consistency. I always answer her question with a question before making my final decision: "How much?" The price scanners on the wall are my best friend as I tend to make decisions based on budget, not design.

With much more serious implications, Jesus challenged bystanders who asked to follow him to first consider the cost before committing. To follow Jesus is a decision that supersedes all others. To provide clarity on the thought process of a committed follower, he likened the decision to building a tower. Just like a builder must estimate construction costs and budget appropriately, we should count the cost when making commitments.

Here are some tips we can extract from this parable to help us be better budgeters when making decisions as leaders.

Application

1. Budget before building: This is basic but failed so often as we would rather fantasize over interior decorations and finishes than crunch numbers. You must budget the price of your dreams to avoid going bankrupt. Are you willing to pay the price? Leaders begin with the end in mind.
2. Don't forget the hidden costs: Sticker prices never paint an accurate picture. We must consider taxes, fees, and other costs. Success may cost you things that are not seen at surface-level analysis.
3. Weigh the cost of no: While following Jesus was costly, the alternative was unaffordable. What would be the consequences of saying no to your God-given dreams and responsibilities? Who would suffer from your no?

Supplication

God, give me the precision of an accountant when making business and leadership choices. Help me accurately assess the cost of my decisions and budget accordingly. Thank you for covering the ultimate cost that I could not afford so that I may have life eternally. Amen.

Implementation

Take some time to consider what your dreams are and write down the necessary steps and sacrifices required to accomplish your dreams. Are you willing to pay that price?

_____

_____

_____

_____

_____

_____

_____

Day 5

Service

/sur-vis/
n. a helpful act

Information

> *Do to others as you would have them do to you.*
>
> —Luke 6:31 NIV

"Your call is very important to us, please remain on the line and the next available representative will be with you shortly." I'm sure I am not the only one who has been on hold for over an hour while listening to this message about how important my call is. Have you ever been on hold for so long that you wanted to throw the phone across the room? Have you ever pressed every number on the keypad and still got a robot instead of a human? Despite the millions of dollars companies invest in training, many businesses and organizations still fail miserably when providing service to customers. The reason is that many of them don't consider the most important thing ... the customer. If you don't enjoy being on hold for hours, chances are, your customers don't either.

While I could write a novel on customer service, I'll spare you the time and keep it simple. Luke gives us the key to stellar service—treat people the way you want to be treated. Jesus built his kingdom around this idea and told his followers that they would be identified not by their name tags but by the way they loved each other.

I hope that we as Christian leaders in the marketplace would build organizations that serve so intensely that the world stops and stares. If you aspire to build a brand like this, follow these next three steps.

Application

1. Show empathy: Others don't care how much you know until they know how much you care. Putting yourself in their shoes is the first step to responding properly.
2. Own your mistakes: Be sure to admit your flaws instead of masking them. The willingness to take responsibility fosters an environment of trust both internally with our team and externally with our customers.
3. Be kind: This should go without saying, but be nice. Always strive to make a friend when servicing people. People may forget what you said, but they won't forget how you made them feel.

Supplication

Father, help me to treat those around me the way I would like to be treated. I pray for guidance as I serve customers and interact with my team members so that my action would be God-honoring. Amen.

Implementation

What can you do to ensure that you and those you lead are serving your customers well?

_____

_____

_____

_____

_____

_____

_____

Day 6

Skill

/skil/
n. the ability to use one's knowledge effectively and readily in execution or performance

Information

If the ax is dull and its edge unsharpened, more strength is needed, but skill will bring success.

—Ecclesiastes 10:10 NIV

"You are doing it all wrong," my father exclaimed on a hot Texas summer day. However, this was not the first time I heard those words. I was swinging with all of my might, trying to chop down a modest tree in our yard, yet it remained upright. Swing by swing, I channeled my inner lumberjack, but it was not until my dad stepped in that the tree hit the ground.

He began to show me the proper way to chop down trees with an ax, and in doing so, he gave me the ingredients for creating success in life. First, he pointed out that I had hit the tree from the root to the branches and explained the importance of hitting the tree in the same spot. My dad then proceeded to restore the sharpness of my dull blade. With a sharp blade and a few well-aimed swings, the tree tumbled.

Life goals can be much like chopping trees. I've noticed in my own businesses that I'm much more effective when I take the time to become proficient. The things that used to keep me up at night are now simple tasks that can be completed with ease because of learned competence. Every leader can extract the following from this story to tackle their next goal.

Application

1. Heed advice: If I had kept doing things my way, I would have remained exhausted and frustrated. Only after I deferred to experience was I able to understand the pattern of success. Success always leaves clues if you will listen.

2. Fix your aim: I used at least three times the amount of energy required to chop down the tree and accomplished very little. Contrarily, my dad struck the tree with discipline and achieved the goal. Keep your organization on task and focused.

3. Sharpen your ax: Famously attributed to Abraham Lincoln is the quote, "If I had an hour to chop down a tree, I would spend the first 45 minutes sharpening my ax." In your business, be certain you aren't swinging a dull ax just to appear busy. Make sure that your efforts are making progress towards the intended outcome.

Supplication

Father, give me the wisdom to work smarter, not harder. I pray for the discernment to recognize when my methods are inefficient and for the discipline to strike with accuracy. Amen.

Implementation

Consider—what skills can you develop that will make your operation more efficient?

_____

_____

_____

_____

_____

_____

_____

Day 7

Posture

/**pos**-cher/
n. a conscious mental or outward behavioral attitude

Information

Suddenly a furious storm came up on the lake so that the waves swept over the boat. But Jesus was sleeping.

—Matthew 8:24 NIV

"We interrupt this program to bring you an important message." ABC, NBC, CNN, and Fox were for once all saying the same thing. Heck, even ESPN was talking about this event. In the blink of an eye, normal as we knew it ceased to exist due to the Covid-19 pandemic. What would we do if our 2,000 tenants stopped paying? How will we lease our properties? Will we keep our jobs? All were questions to which my team expected answers. I was a 24-year-old newly appointed President who was preparing to address my team the next morning to discuss plans for problems our nation's brightest and most experienced leaders did not have total solutions for. I prayed, stayed up all night, and then presented "operation shutdown" to our team. Our intensive hands-on operation was now 95% online overnight.

We still managed to fill up our property and collect 99% of the expected rent ... from home.

At that moment I felt like I was in a storm with no clear end in sight, but that was not the most important thing. The most important thing was my response. While the severity of the storm matters, the posture of a leader during the problem is critical to mission success. Despite the fierce storm in Matthew 8, Jesus was found sleeping soundly. The disciples were restless, and Jesus was resting. They were fear-filled; he was faith-filled. Sometimes the posture of the leader will determine whether proverbial winds in life dissipate or waves overtake.

I'm no Jesus, but I learned from his approach to problems. Leaders must be able to provide calmness in chaos and arrangement to the abstract. Here's some chiropractic help to correct your leadership posture.

Application

1. Remain calm: While the disciples were crying and running, Jesus was calm and confident. As a leader, your posture is always being observed by those who follow you, so you must consider the message you are sending. Does your posture exude faith and confidence in Christ or fear because of uncertainty?

2. Educate yourself: Jesus was able to respond differently because he had more information. The disciples marveled when Jesus took control of the winds with his voice, but Jesus knew that was in him the whole time, allowing him to respond differently. Staying in God's word allows us to have the right response to the world's issues.

3. Respond from the inside: If you allow outside circumstances to control inward emotions, you'll never be stable, as change is inevitable. As Christians, when the world presents us with problems, we should respond from the spirit of power on the inside of us.

Supplication

Father, when there are storms in my life, I know that you control the winds with the sound of your voice. Help me to be a leader of faith who doesn't panic during the pandemonium. Amen.

Implementation

Consider a time when your posture as a leader impacted those around you. What can you do to make sure you exude confidence in Christ during times of turmoil?

_____

_____

_____

_____

_____

_____

Day 8

Trust

/truhst/
n. assured reliance on the character, ability, strength, or truth of someone or something

Information

The Lord had said to Abram, "Go from your country, your people and your father's household to the land I will show you."

—Genesis 12:1 NIV

We had a bit of sleep in our eyes, and the fog was still hovering slightly above the pavement as we loaded into our rental van. Despite the early hour, we were filled with excitement and anticipation. My cousins and I were finally headed to the promised land, or at least the land promised to us by our grandparents—Disney! For years we dreamed about meeting Mickey Mouse and experiencing the "happiest place on earth." We embarked on this exciting road trip only to have our energy dissipated by the arduous journey. Disney was 850 miles of straight highway from my small hometown in Louisiana. The more we traveled, the more we questioned my grandparents on if we were close yet. One hour, two hours, and 10 hours passed, and we still were not there. My grandparents continued to assure us that there would be no question when we arrived. We would know when we reached Disney.

I imagine this is how Abram felt when God gave him vague directions to a land he would show him, not one he had shown him. Abram set out in faith and trusted God for more direction as he journeyed. God is much like a GPS in the fact that he sometimes gives instructions like, "Continue straight for 100 miles" and then remains silent for 99 miles until it is time for a turn or exit. For Abram to be the father of many nations, he had to leave his father's house in faith. Today, Abraham's lineage continues to reap the rewards of his obedience.

God normally won't give you more direction until you obey what he has already spoken. Here are some practical steps to help you venture into the unknown, especially as you lead others in uncertainty.

Application

1. Act on what you know: We often wait for the complete picture before we are willing to obey, but that is not faith. Trust in what God has spoken and walk in faith.
2. Follow directions: Do not create chaos for the sake of excitement. If God has not told you to exit, stay on track. He is faithful and will speak when you are close to pivotal moments.
3. Check your music: If you have not heard God speak, one of two things is happening. Either you are on the right path, or your music is too loud, drowning out God's instructions. Don't let the many voices in the world cloud the voice of God.

Supplication

God, give me faith to leave the familiar. Help me to trust and obey the words you have spoken over my life, even when I don't completely understand. Amen.

Implementation

Where do you presently feel God directing you, and what voices do you need to turn down so that you can hear God clearly?

_____

_____

_____

_____

_____

_____

_____

Day 9

Empower

/em-**pou**-er/
v. give official authority or legal power to

Information

I will give you the keys of the kingdom of heaven; whatever you bind on earth will be bound in heaven, and whatever you loose on earth will be loosed in heaven.

—Matthew 16:19 NIV

It's been over 2,000 years since the death of Christ, who lived on earth for just 33 years, yet we are still talking about him today. Countless others have walked this earth much longer than Jesus did; however, none have left the footprint he did, not even the greatest philosophers of their respective eras. This is in part due to the deity of Christ, but I think there is also something to be said about his strategic planning. Many leaders fail to plan their departures, so their missions die when they do. They fail to pass on their secret recipe, trade secrets, and core functions. For a vision to outlive the visionary, others must be empowered.

In preparation for this physical departure, Christ equipped other leaders to continue his mission throughout all generations. He gave someone else the keys to make moves that would impact his kingdom in heaven and on earth. Today, the ministry of Christ lives on in all of us who have received his spirit.

Organizations that are built to last distribute power to those within the organization. Jesus had a clear exit plan in place before he departed the earth. Below are steps for empowering other leaders.

Application

1. Do it: To teach, you must have a clear understanding. This comes through perfecting your craft.
2. Do it with someone: Once you have learned a skill, bring someone along and teach them.
3. Supervise them doing it: Once a skill is taught, allow them to do it while you supervise and give guidance.
4. Empower with freedom: After trust is earned, empower your people with freedom and autonomy. Let them do it.
5. Repeat: Leaders create leaders. Your trainee should repeat the process and continue the model of replication within the organization. Trainees must become trainers. This is what we call discipleship.

Supplication

Father, I pray for your guidance to disciple others in a way that glorifies you. I entrust to you the things that you have given me stewardship over, and I ask that you'd empower me to empower others to lead in my absence. Amen.

Implementation

List at least one person you have identified as an up-and-coming leader. What can you do to help develop that person?

_____

_____

_____

_____

_____

_____

_____

Day 10

Resourceful

/ri-**sawrs**-fuhl/
adj. able to meet situations: capable of devising ways and means

Information

> *Here is a boy with five small barley loaves and two small fish, but how far will they go among so many?*
>
> —John 6:9 NIV

I drove away from the duplexes thrilled that I had finally found a "deal." I probably broke a few speed limit laws as I hurried to my mentor's home to tell him the good news. I explained the property to him at his dining room table, and he confirmed what I suspected; this property was a steal! But there was just one problem … I didn't have $500,000 to buy it. Despite my financial limitations, he challenged me to make the offer anyhow. He assured me that with a stellar deal, the money would show up. I had limited financial resources but a lot of resourcefulness. I was able to acquire that purchase and millions of dollars more with no money out of my pocket because I used the things that I did have—passion, thirst, drive, and discipline.

Similarly, Jesus challenged two of his mentees, Phillip and Andrew, with feeding 5,000 plus with just two small fish and five loaves. Phillip, when challenged, could only see the lack of resources and capital readily available to feed such a large crowd. He knew that even with half a year's wages he could only buy enough food for each person to get a bite-sized sample. Andrew was a little more resourceful, finding a young boy with a small meal, but Andrew felt that his product was no match for the problem. Contrarily, Jesus showed great things can come from small beginnings by feeding the 5,000 and collecting leftovers.

There are many points we can glean from this story that still reign true today. Here are a few things that we can learn from Jesus' miracle.

Application

1. Trust the source, not resources: Philip was focused on the lack of resources, and Andrew was focused on the size of the resources. Jesus focused his attention on the source.
2. Prepare for provision: Jesus created order by having the people sit in rows before eating. He was preparing for something special. If you expect something great to happen, prepare for it.
3. Give thanks: Instead of complaining about what he lacked, Jesus gave thanks for what he had. What seemingly small things can you be grateful for today?

Supplication

Father, I thank you for days of small beginnings. I give you praise for every seed planted in my life, and I pray that you provide an increase. You are a God that produces great things from small starts. Amen.

Implementation

What resource in your life that may seem small have you taken for granted? How can you surrender it to God?

Day 11

Responsibility

*/ri-spon-suh-**bil**-i-tee/*
n. state of being accountable or trustworthy:
such as moral accountability

Information

Then David said to Nathan, "I have sinned against the Lord."

—2 Samuel 12:13 NIV

The man said, "The woman you put here with me—she gave me fruit from the tree and I ate it."

—Genesis 3:12 NIV

My cousin and I were awkwardly quiet when my mom returned home from work that afternoon. She knew something was wrong, but she couldn't quite place her finger on it—that is, until she sat in her normal spot on the couch. When my mother sat down, her once sturdy couch leaned back like a recliner. She immediately screamed, "Who did it?" Refusing to take responsibility, I pointed at my cousin. I had slammed him into the couch, but I blamed him for provoking me into anger. It was his fault that I tackled him! How silly does that sound?

Ironically, many adults respond similarly. Adam, when questioned by God about his mistake, blamed his wife and God before himself. He deflected blame by mentioning his role in the mistake last. Contrarily, David, known as a man after God's own heart, accepted his downfalls many times. Granted, he had a bunch of practice, but he owned his faults, nonetheless.

God can work with and through those who are transparent about their mistakes, not those who blame others. Below are the keys to being a leader who takes ownership.

Application

1. Always use "I" when accepting fault: Leaders don't blame others and circumstances for their faults. They point the finger at themselves.
2. Look internally, not externally: Instead of analyzing all the things around you that went wrong, analyze what happened inside of you that led to your mistake.
3. Learn from your mistakes: It is important that as you take accountability, you don't allow your mistakes to become a habit. Looking back at what we did wrong is not for us to dwell on the shortcomings of the past but to learn from them so we don't repeat those same actions.

Supplication

Father, keep me reminded of my humanity and imperfection. Help me to humbly accept that I am not perfect so that I can make progress toward perfection. Amen.

Implementation

What is something that you might've blamed on others in the past that you feel you need to take ownership for?

_____

_____

_____

_____

_____

_____

_____

Day 12

Action

*/**ak**-shuhn/*
n. a thing done

Information

> *Whoever watches the wind will not plant; whoever looks at the clouds will not reap.*
>
> —Ecclesiastes 11:4 NIV

Due to the advancements in technology and access to real-time weather updates, we don't have to be as attentive to nature as Old Testament farmers. The livelihoods of farmers are dependent upon their seeds producing a harvest, so it is fitting that they would want to plant their crops at the most opportune time possible. However, Solomon was wise enough to recognize that there will never appear to be a perfect time to plant a seed, and those who don't plant won't reap.

Sometimes, we have to act in faith and leave the forecast to our Father. After all, the winds and waves obey his commands. Maybe you aren't a farmer planting corn, but I bet there are seeds you are holding in your hand for the perfect time. Maybe it is a book, business, or even a church God has placed in your heart to plant, but you have been waiting for the right wind conditions.

If you have a God-given idea and you have received a green light from the Holy Spirit that it is time to plant, my advice is the same as Nike's ... just do it. You can always adjust, but missed opportunities are just that, missed. Here's how you can avoid procrastination and pursue purpose.

Application

1. Know that God's word trumps winds: If God has spoken over your life, the things that he said will not return void. Even when conditions seem poor, God can still fulfill his purpose in your life.
2. Plant to prosper: If you never sow, you'll never reap. You must act. Will you go to work or watch the wind?
3. Trust God's will: While it is our job to plant, we are not in charge of the increase. God oversees the outcome from our efforts, and his timing is always perfect.

Supplication

When the winds worry me, help to focus on the God who has power over the winds. Father, help me to not watch the wind but to get to work. Amen.

Implementation

List something that you have been wanting to do, but you've been waiting for the perfect time. How can you begin to act on that idea now?

_____

_____

_____

Action

_____
_____
_____
_____

Day 13

Humility

*/hyoo-**mil**-i-tee/*
n. freedom from pride or arrogance

Information

> *One day as Jesus was standing by the Lake of Gennesaret, the people were crowding around him and listening to the word of God. He saw at the water's edge two boats, left there by the fishermen, who were washing their nets. When he had finished speaking, he said to Simon, "Put out into deep water, and let down the nets for a catch." Simon answered, "Master, we've worked hard all night and haven't caught anything. But because you say so, I will let down the nets." When they had done so, they caught such a large number of fish that their nets began to break. So they signaled their partners in the other boat to come and help them, and they came and filled both boats so full that they began to sink.*
>
> —Luke 5:1–2, 4–7 NIV

"Why?" I asked. "Because I said so," replied my mother. This was the answer I dreaded most as it did not seem sufficient to a stubborn kid like me. Growing up, I was not the respectful person I am today. The kid being spanked in the cereal aisle at

Walmart, that was me. One surefire way to summon a good spanking was to talk back to my momma, and, boy, did my mouth get me in trouble. It took me a while to realize that our house was not a democracy with checks and balances where it was hard to formalize action. I grew up in an autocracy where power was concentrated in the voice of one person. When momma spoke, everything shifted.

Similarly, the life of Simon and his crew was completely changed by one voice. Jesus showed up on his boat, spoke, and changed everything. The fisherman used the same boat, bait, and nets. Jesus' voice was the only new variable introduced into the experiment. Jesus "said so" and that was enough to make their nets go from empty to overflowing.

Simon's humility allowed him to set aside his own expertise and listen to someone he trusted. This simple act of humility radically changed the outcome of his fishing trip. He was willing to try again, heed instruction, and share the abundance he received.

Likewise, we can all learn from this example and let humility be a transformative force in our lives and leadership. Let's explore the powerful applications from this text for the life of a leader.

Application

1. Try again: The fishermen were washing their nets, which signaled that they were done. Sometimes, when we are done and have exhausted all that we know, Jesus is just getting started. Whenever Jesus speaks a word in your life, obey.

2. Listen to trusted advisors: These guys were professional fishermen who were not too proud to take directions. They had experience coupled with all of the right analytics, but God's voice transcended all human logic. Every great leader knows how to follow the voice of God.

3. Share: The catch was so great that they had to signal for their partners. Did you know that your obedience could be tied to someone else's well-being?

Supplication

Father, your voice is the voice the one that spoke the world into existence, and it is that same voice that can change my existence in this world. Give me wisdom to obey, humility to listen, and generosity to share. Amen.

Implementation

What is something you tried and failed in the past that you now see as a potential opportunity, if you find the right advisors?

_____

_____

_____

_____

_____

_____

_____

Day 14

Depend

/dih-***pend***/
v. to place reliance or trust

Information

Moses answered, "What if they do not believe me or listen to me and say, 'The Lord did not appear to you?'" Then the Lord said to him, "What is that in your hand?" "A staff," he replied.

—Exodus 4:1–2 NIV

My eyes locked with the fear-filled eyes of my wife, and terror spread throughout the room after hearing the loud voice. We held our breath to not make a sound and tip the intruder to our location within our home. Within seconds, I went from fear to fighting mode. It was my moment to protect our house. While I was reaching for the bedroom door, my intelligent wife asked if I was going to take a weapon with me. I reached for my .380 and found that I had left it in the truck. With no other option, I reached for a candle and contemplated lighting it to elevate it into a flamethrower. While having this ridiculous sitcom-worthy internal dialogue, I received the idea to use what was at my disposal. Thankfully, no one was on the other side of the door, and God was just giving me good sermon material. The audible voice we heard was that of the neighbors' loud intercom that had started and stopped suddenly, mimicking the voice of a person.

I brought a candle to a gun fight, and I imagine Moses felt as ill-prepared as I did when God called him from 40 years of obscurity to lead the nation of Israel from Egyptian captivity. On the verge of a mental breakdown, Moses questioned God stating, "Who am I, that I should go unto Pharaoh, and that I should bring forth the children of Israel out of Egypt?" Amid Moses' complaining, God asked him a simple yet profound question: "What's in your hand?" It was with the staff that Moses would use to part the red sea, call water from a rock, and defeat the Amalekites. God showed Moses that little is much when God is in it.

In the same fashion, God can do many great things in our lives when we are dependent upon his power, no matter the odds. Here's what we can learn from Moses' interaction with God.

Application

1. Shift your perspective: Moses was so focused on what he lacked that he forgot what he packed. Instead of focusing on the God of the universe, he chose to focus on his inadequacies. It is critical that we focus on the God of the universe and rely on him as our source.
2. Know God is with you: The most important part of the scripture was not what Moses held in his hand, but it was who held his hand. Knowing that God is with you should give you confidence as you lead others.
3. Surrender your hand: Moses had to go from being self-dependent to God-dependent. When you are willing to submit your staff or leadership to Christ, greatness can happen. If you try and do it with your strength, you'll forever be inadequate.

Supplication

Almighty God, I humbly submit the things in my hand for your glory. You are a God who can magnify the meager and transform the ordinary. Use me for your name's sake. Amen.

Implementation

What area in your life do you feel ill-equipped for as a leader that you need to develop greater dependence on God?

_____

_____

_____

_____

_____

_____

_____

Day 15

Focus

/ foh-kuhs /
v. to concentrate attention or effort

Information

> "Come," he said. Then Peter got down out of the boat, walked on the water and came toward Jesus. But when he saw the wind, he was afraid and, beginning to sink, cried out, "Lord, save me!"
>
> —Matthew 14:29–30 NIV

Do you recall the enchantment of visiting the circus as a child? Among all the captivating circus performances, the lion tamer left the most indelible impression to me. Witnessing a 400-pound beast with a roar that shakes the jungle be humbled into submission was mind-blowing. Most lion tamers follow the method of Clyde Beatty, who became renowned for his uncanny method of corralling the king of the jungle by waving a chair in its face. It was with a small stool that Clyde rendered the beast powerless. When the chair was in the face of the beast, it would try and focus on all four legs simultaneously. With its focus divided, the lion would become confused and essentially paralyzed.

In a similar vein, Peter experienced a loss of power when his focus wavered. He managed to stay above water when his eyes were locked on Jesus. However, he sank when he took his eyes off Jesus and fixated on the strong winds and waves. Undoubtedly, Peter likely saw the crashing waves before he began to sink, but the pivotal moment was when he decided to consciously concentrate on them. The same elements that Peter triumphed over while maintaining his gaze had the potential to engulf him when he became distracted.

If you're going to lead well, it requires focus. Below are tips to help you stay locked in on the things and the one who matters.

Application

1. Fix your focus: Are you worried about the wind or focused on Jesus? It is important to recognize what's important and align your focus and priorities accordingly. Circumstances in life will vary, but if you can keep your focus rooted in faith, you'll walk in victory.
2. Identify distractions: Take note of the factors that commonly derail you from achieving your objectives. By recognizing these potential deterrents, you can actively anticipate and address them.
3. Have confidence in his call: If Jesus calls you to it, he will lead you through it. Jesus told Peter to come. His word alone is enough to produce confidence in your ability to walk in divine calling.

Supplication

Father, when the world around me is raging, help me to stay focused on you. Help me to trust your call and walk confidently toward you. Amen.

Implementation

What are some things that you notice often distract you from operating in your calling? What can you do to remain focused and identify those distractions proactively?

_____

_____

_____

_____

_____

_____

_____

Day 16

Tenacious

/tuh-**ney**-shuhs/
adj. persistent in seeking something valued or desired

Information

Here a great number of disabled people used to lie—the blind, the lame, the paralyzed. One who was there had been an invalid for thirty-eight years. When Jesus saw him lying there and learned that he had been in this condition for a long time, he asked him, "Do you want to get well?"

—John 5:3–6 NIV

"Son, you're exactly where you want to be!" My dad chose to abruptly interrupt my conversation with my mom, say his piece, and hang up. I guess it is safe to say that he was tired of me complaining about hard classes and injuries during my time at Texas A&M. While my hardships were real, my dad refused to allow me to make my bed in misery. Left to fill in the blanks of his powerful one-liner, I learned that my dad was correct. I had no right to complain about my situation if I wasn't going to make take the necessary steps to change it.

If I wanted better grades and greater playing time, I needed to prove my desire by implementing the right disciplines.

This experience with my dad made John 5 personal to me. It is here we see a man who had been lame for 38 years get asked a seemingly harsh question by Jesus: "Do you want to get well?" I imagine this inquiry caused the man to observe and reflect on the level of desire he had for healing. Had he done everything he could to get better? Was he ready for the responsibility that would follow his healing? No longer would he benefit from the sympathy that sickness often draws; he'd have to work.

Sometimes, you might find yourself in a long-standing situation where you feel stuck, defeated, and lacking motivation. It is in these moments when you can grow your character and leadership by examining the level of tenacity you are exhibiting and making the necessary changes below that will strengthen your tenacity.

Application

1. Change your environment: This man surrounded himself with other sick people. If you want to excel professionally, you must surround yourself with the right people and culture.

2. Accept responsibility: For 38 years this man was accustomed to the attention that his affliction attracted, but healing would introduce a new obligation in his life. He would no longer be able to beg for a living; he would be called to action. Leaders must embrace the work that accompanies their positions.

3. Ignore opinions: When the lame man began to walk in his healing, the religious leaders criticized him for carrying his mat on the Sabbath. When you start to rise above your circumstances, there will be naysayers. It is crucial that you disregard negativity and continue to walk victoriously.

Supplication

Father, ignite a desire for growth and development in my heart. Do not allow me to succumb to excuses for my condition but grant me unwavering tenacity to overcome with you as my guide. Amen.

Implementation

Are there any areas in your life where you feel stuck or stagnant? If so, what can you do to align your actions with your desire to create meaningful progress?

_____

_____

_____

_____

_____

_____

_____

Day 17

Gratitude

*/**grat**-i-tood /*
n. the state of being grateful

Information

> *One of them, when he saw he was healed, came back, praising God in a loud voice. He threw himself at Jesus' feet and thanked him—and he was a Samaritan. Jesus asked, "Were not all ten cleansed? Where are the other nine? Has no one returned to give praise to God except this foreigner?" Then he said to him, "Rise and go; your faith has made you well."*
>
> —Luke 17:15–19 NIV

Van Gogh could not have painted a more beautiful sunset than the one we experienced that night over Brooke Lake. The water was still, the breeze perfect, and the fish were biting. I was granted the privilege, via a mutual friend, of fishing with my teammates in the backyard of a house belonging to a man who had done something well in life, judging from the looks of his home. I saw this man exit his backdoor, and it all began to make sense. The behemoth of a person was obviously a retired NBA player. I paddled my way across the lake to thank him for his hospitality, and an amazing conversation about his real estate career followed. He turned out not to be Larry Bird, but a real estate entrepreneur. That simple thank you was the catalyst to a business partnership that neither of us saw coming.

When I read about the grateful leper, I can't help but think about the night I met my first business partner. From his recollection, I was the only player that took the time to greet and thank him. I say this not to cast a negative light on anyone else, but to illustrate the power of gratitude.

How often do we neglect to give thanks for the many blessings we have in life? How often do we accept the gift without recognizing the giver? If you want to be someone of impact and influence, begin by being grateful for where you are.

Application

1. Recognize what you've been given: Many times, when we decide to be more grateful, we think of it as a future activity. Take the time now to be thankful for what you currently have.
2. Never neglect the giver: Every gift is tied to a giver. Do not get so enthralled with what you have received that you forget who gave it to you.
3. Practice it daily: Gratitude is like showering—do it daily. Researchers continue to echo the many positive effects of gratitude. Each one of those benefits grows as we practice gratitude more often.

Supplication

God, I just want to come before you today to say thank you. You are enough, and if you never do anything else for me, I am grateful for what you have already done. Amen.

Implementation

Take some time to consider and write down what you are presently grateful for.

_____

_____

_____

_____

_____

_____

_____

Day 18

Brand

/brand/
n. a public image, reputation, or identity conceived of as something to be marketed or promoted

Information

A new command I give you: Love one another. As I have loved you, so you must love one another. By this, everyone will know that you are my disciples, if you love one another.

—John 13:34–35 NIV

The quiet shyness of the incoming freshman in the locker room turned into rambunctious cockiness when prodded by the upperclassmen. They all wanted the upperclassmen to believe they were "somebody." I quietly observed arguments about star rankings and stats, and I must admit their credentials were a little intimidating for me as an unknown and unranked recruit playing a new position. In the days to come, my position coach could tell I was a little concerned, but he eased those concerns with one statement: "Sez, film don't lie." That statement was true! It did not matter how many stars I had; the only thing that mattered was my performance between the white lines. If I wanted to earn a spot on the field, all I had to do was perform.

This is exactly what Jesus told his disciples when announcing his departure. His disciples would become known by their actions, in particular, how they loved each other. Their brand would be what they displayed. If they had the desire to be identified as Christ-followers, they needed to act like Christ. Simply put, he told them that people would know them by what they showed them.

As a leader, your actions must match your words. The quickest way to erode trust is to talk about things you don't put into action. If you want to build a powerful brand, turn your attention toward today's application.

Application

1. Talk less: The book of Proverbs says that "mere talk leads to poverty." You don't get to talk your way into building a brand; you must back it up with action. You must show the things you'd like to be known for.
2. Cultivate your values: It is crucial to establish a set of core values or character traits that you consider non-negotiable. By steadfastly upholding these core principles, they become ingrained within your identity and recognized by others.
3. Be consistent: Branding is not something that you do once, it is what you do habitually. You must show up each day ready to give it your best.

Supplication

Father, help me to behave in a way that is representative of who you are. I pray that men will see my good work and give glory to you. Amen.

Implementation

How do you want to be remembered and what can you do to display that brand?

_____

_____

_____

_____

_____

_____

_____

Day 19

Profit

/prof-it/
n. a valuable return

Information

> *"So I was afraid and went out and hid your gold in the ground. See, here is what belongs to you." His master replied, "You wicked, lazy servant! So you knew that I harvest where I have not sown and gather where I have not scattered seed? Well then, you should have put my money on deposit with the bankers, so that when I returned I would have received it back with interest."*
>
> —Matthew 25:25–27 NIV

That's the one!" my business partner shouted. "That's the one!" We had spent the entire day driving through neighborhoods, calling realtors, and looking for something to buy. Unfortunately, we were not the only people looking to buy a house, and all the good ones seemed to be taken. I had seen some stunning houses that day, and to my surprise, my partner was most excited about an old beat-up house with overgrown grass, peeling paint, and a leaking roof. Fast forward a few years and it all makes sense. We look for the worst house in the best neighborhood. These houses normally offer the greatest financial reward and consistently meet our most important metric, ROI or return on investment. We do not invest for beauty or emotion; we invest for returns.

Matthew 25 so eloquently illustrates this principle and gives us a guide on avoiding financial and spiritual bankruptcy. The master entrusted his wealth to three workers. The first two proved their fruitfulness and provided a 100% return on the master's investment. Like with any good investment, he decided to put more of his resources into them. Contrarily, the last servant was treated harshly because he hid the master's money and produced no return on his capital.

I think it is important for us to recognize that God expects a return on everything he has placed inside of us. If you want to ensure you produce a return as a leader, the following application is for you.

Application

1. Fear not: Each worker was gifted according to his ability. If God has given you something, that means you have the capacity to develop and utilize that gift.
2. Realize you are gifted: Some people go their whole lives not realizing what they have been given. You are gifted.
3. Produce returns: We will all be measured by what we do with what has been entrusted to us. Investments are measured by the return they produce.

Supplication

God, I recognize that with gifting comes responsibility. I pray that you would grant me the courage to utilize what you've gifted me. Amen.

Implementation

Jot down some ways in which you are uniquely gifted and how you can maximize what God has gifted with you.

_____

_____

_____

_____

_____

_____

_____

Day 20

Rooted

*/**roo**-tid/*
adj. established deeply and firmly

Information

I am the vine; you are the branches. If you remain in me and I in you, you will bear much fruit; apart from me you can do nothing.

—John 15:5 NIV

Whenever we moved into our first home my wife became a self-proclaimed "plant lady." She loves an aesthetic neutral pallet with pops of earth tones and greenery. Admittedly, she had some learning to do when she first started—may those plants rest in peace. During the early days, we were buying all kinds of plants, gardening tools, and fertilizer to enhance our growing greenhouse. Keeping with that theme, my wife decided to bring home a free centerpiece of exotic flowers from a charity function. It was not long after this that I saw her disposing of those flowers, and I jokingly asked if she had killed another one. However, this one was not the same, and it was not her fault. This plant died because it was disconnected from its roots.

In my life and business experiences, I've seen many leaders perish because of the same reason. When we become prideful and believe that we are self-made, we fail. To flourish, we must be connected to our power source and vine. For the believer, that vine is Christ. Apart from him, we are nothing but pretty decorations with no life source, waiting to be disposed of. The stark contrasting reality is that with Christ all things are possible, and apart from him we can do nothing of lasting value.

Yes, you might build something that appears beautiful, but the end of it is destruction if it isn't rooted in Christ. If you want to live a life filled with fruitfulness that lasts, here's how you do it.

Application

1. Abide in the Lord: Much like a phone plugged into a power cord, you must stay plugged into Christ if you want to produce power. We should rely on Christ as our daily bread. Remain in him.
2. Be pruned: Allow Christ to trim back the areas in your life that are not conducive to growth. We must want there to be less of us and more of him.
3. Bear fruit: The purpose of every plant is to produce and grow. The byproduct of abiding in Christ is that you should produce fruit. Resting in him leads to results.

Supplication

Christ, it is in you that we live, move, and have our being. Help me to abide in your grace and faithfulness. Allow me to stay tethered to you and always acknowledge you as the source of my strength. Amen.

Implementation

What actions can you take to remain firmly rooted in Gospel-centered living and leadership? How do you plan to implement those actions into your daily routine?

_____

_____

_____

_____

_____

_____

_____

Day 21

Promotion

/pruh-**moh**-shuhn/
n. act of being raised in position or rank

Information

> From the time He put him in charge of his household and of all he owned, the Lord blessed the household of the Egyptian because of Joseph. The blessing of the Lord was on everything Potiphar had, both in the house and in the field. So Potiphar left everything he had in Joseph's care; with Joseph in charge, he did not concern himself with anything except the food he ate.
>
> —Genesis 39:5–6 NIV

Ray Lewis once said that "greatness is a bunch of small things done well." Often when we think of greatness, game-winning drives, no-hitters, and big deals come to mind. We don't think of small, mundane consistency when the word "greatness" comes to mind, but small things done well are exactly what leads to greatness.

While I did become the president of multiple organizations by the age of 24, I can't take credit for the blueprint that I used. I followed biblical role models and demonstrated things like punctuality, meticulous attention to details, and genuine concern for others. Joseph perfectly modeled how to be promoted in his service to Potiphar. Joseph was sold into slavery by his jealous brothers and landed in the house of Potiphar, an Egyptian captain. While in Potiphar's house, he quickly rose the ranks and became the head of Potiphar's affairs.

The good thing for you is that success always leaves clues or a roadmap. Here's how Joseph became deserving of promotion and how you can do it.

Application

1. Make the best of every situation: You may have skimmed over this, but Joseph was sold into slavery by his brothers. If anyone had the right to complain, it was Joseph. Instead, he took a lemon and made lemonade.

2. Do your job well: If you want another position, you must excel where you are. Joseph was promoted after Potiphar observed his excellence, not because Joseph complained about a promotion. Rulers over many are first faithful in few.

3. Make your team better: Joseph not only bettered the house of Potiphar, but he also increased performance in the field. Leaders bring out the best in those around them. Joseph's attitude of excellence rippled throughout Potiphar's estate.

4. Build freedom for your boss: When your boss is only concerned with what he or she is having for lunch, you know you are doing a good job. The more you can provide in value, the more you will be compensated.

Supplication

Father, help me to give more in value than I am presently compensated for. Help me to bring the best out in those around me and honor every situation you place me in with excellent stewardship. Amen.

Implementation

What routine activities can you display excellence in that would lead to greater leadership opportunities in the future? How will this not only benefit you, but those in your sphere of influence?

_____

_____

_____

_____

_____

_____

Day 22

Secure

/si-**kyoor**/
adj. assured in expectation: having no doubt

Information

Jesus' mother and brothers came to see him, but they were not able to get near him because of the crowd.

—Luke 8:19 NIV

Then everyone deserted him and fled.

—Mark 14:50 NIV

Never has the spirit of "cancel culture" been as high as it is today. With the increased presence of social media, we now have visibility into the lives of many people whom we don't know personally, giving us the freedom to be more critical of them. I experienced this phenomenon when playing college sports. My performance was viewed and criticized by millions every week. Depending on the week, I was either on the top of a mountain or at the bottom of a valley as passionate collegiate fans expressed their love/hate relationship with me. One week fancypants23 praised me on the message boards, and other weeks footballdiva87 questioned if I should even be on the team.

In our text above we see "cancel culture" taking a shot at Jesus. During the miracle season of Jesus' life, his family couldn't even get to him through all the paparazzi. Fans were tearing off roofs, climbing trees, and crawling on the ground to get to Jesus. However, nearing his life's purpose and moment of suffering, they all deserted him and fled. Despite his many viral moments, he found himself unfollowed when companionship was needed most. Jesus' cross caused the crowds to diminish. Born to die, breathing his last breath, Jesus was unfollowed.

You can be encouraged by Jesus' life and know that just because everyone isn't singing your praises doesn't mean you aren't in the will of God. It is paramount that you seek God's approval, not the approval of man. Here are some practical steps that will help keep you focused on fulfilling God's call for your life.

Application

1. Commit to calling: You can't attach your purpose to your popularity. In a world where many are chasing a blue check next to their name, Jesus is looking to those who will commit to calling.

2. Keep proper perspective when popular: Remember that life is composed of seasons. Don't allow moments of fame to inflate your perspective and make you arrogant.

3. Know that applause doesn't equal God's approval: It's tempting to measure success by the volume of applause, but Jesus demonstrated on the cross in his most successful moment that sometimes the Father is most proud when no one is singing our praises.

Supplication

Father, give me the strength to pursue your purpose over man's popularity. Help me pursue your vision and not viral moments. May my eyes be distinctly on you in a world so crowded with distractions. Amen.

Implementation

Reflect on the example of Jesus and how he received both adoration and desertion from the crowd. How does this inspire you to avoid seeking validation from people and seek God's approval?

_____

_____

_____

_____

_____

_____

_____

Day 23

Evaluate

/ih-**val**-yoo-eyt/
v. to determine the condition of usually by careful study

Information

And the Lord God called unto Adam, and said unto him, where art thou?

—Genesis 3:9 KJV

If you want to see the magic trick that turns a tough football player into a crying little boy, take me inside a shopping mall. Shopping is undeniably my kryptonite, creating an intriguing dynamic when I accompany my wife who gets energy from "retail therapy." She can aimlessly wander around for hours with no plan. After all, one would not want to miss out on the opportunity of stumbling into a Bath & Body Works sale. Since I hate shopping, I love the directory that allows me to get in and out swiftly by providing directions to my destination. However, without a reference point, directories are useless. The star indicating, "You are here" is critical because if you don't identify where you are in proximity to your destination, you'll never know which way to walk.

Adam, having fallen and sinned is asked a profound, yet simple question by God. God questioned Adam stating, "Where art thou?" God, being omniscient and omnipresent, was well aware of Adam's physical location. The question was raised not to locate Adam's physical coordinates, but to challenge Adam to assess his fallen spiritual nature. For Adam to be restored, he had to be honest about where he was.

Similarly, we must be honest about where we are to get to where we are going. Here's how you can locate yourself to make progress toward your calling.

Application

1. Recognize your location: You must begin with the realization of where you are. Directions to destiny require a starting address.

2. Resolve the problem: Once you have a starting point, you must get to work. Ideas and realizations are great, but execution leads to results. Attack!

3. Rejoice often: Celebrate the small wins of progress. Small wins create momentum.

Supplication

Father, help me to be honest with others and myself when evaluating where I am. I pray for directions to destiny and for a realization of where I am on my journey. Amen.

Implementation

Consider the importance of locating where you are in relation to where you want to be in life. Are there any areas in your life that you need to honestly assess where you are in order to make progress towards accomplishing your goals?

_____

_____

_____

_____

_____

_____

_____

Day 24

Authentic

/aw-**then**-tik/
adj. true to one's God-given personality, spirit, or character

Information

Then Saul dressed David in his own tunic. He put a coat of armor on him and a bronze helmet on his head. David fastened his sword over the tunic and tried walking around, because he was not used to them. "I cannot go in these," he said to Saul, "because I am not used to them." So he took them off.

—1 Samuel 17:38–39 NIV

Throbbing, achy, and sore, my feet were killing me as I limped into the Texas A&M locker room at halftime. Admittedly, the new custom-made uniforms we were wearing in that game elevated my swag, drip, sauce, and whatever other colloquialisms you can use for good looks, but I felt terrible. Upon reaching my locker, I quickly began to dig for my old faithful cleats that had been molded to my feet through much practice. Thankfully, I was able to finish the game strong as the pain began to subside while wearing my familiar cleats.

We see in 1 Samuel 17 that David had to make a similar decision after pleading with Saul to let him fight Goliath on behalf of the nation of Israel. Hesitantly, Saul agreed to let David fight, but not without stipulations. Saul wanted David to look like a "real" warrior fighting Goliath, so he gave him a makeover. After walking around in Saul's bulky armor, the scripture states that David "took it off."

As leaders, we are often laden with expectations from the outside world. David is proof that you can blaze your trail and not follow the commonly traveled road. How many of us need to take off expectations that have been placed on us? If you are in that count, turn your attention to the application.

Application

1. Trust your training: The temptation we face in big moments is to try and be special. However, the same fundamentals that win scrimmages win championships. David understood that if he remained faithful to his training and trusted in God, the giant would face the same fate as the lion and bear he slayed while safeguarding his father's sheep.

2. Take it off: Every now and then, we all need a wardrobe change. We need to take off the expectations of society and lead in the way God called us.

3. Avoid comparison: If David would've gotten stuck comparing himself to King Saul, he would've missed what God was calling him to do. Likewise, it is important that you avoid comparing your calling to others and operate in the space and place God has called you to.

Supplication

Today I pray for the strength to resist the urges to conform to the image the world wants me to be. Lord, help me to be authentic to who you called me to be, ignoring the voices that often cloud clarity. Amen.

Implementation

What are some expectations that have been placed on you by the world that you've felt pressure to conform to? What can you do to overcome these feelings and stay true to the calling of God?

_____

_____

_____

_____

_____

_____

_____

Day 25

Treasure

/trezh-er/
v. to hold or keep as precious

Information

> *Do not store up for yourselves treasures on earth, where moths and vermin destroy, and where thieves break in and steal. But store up for yourselves treasures in heaven, where moths and vermin do not destroy, and where thieves do not break in and steal. For where your treasure is, there your heart will be also.*
>
> —Matthew 6:19-21 NIV

Whenever my in-laws moved closer to our home, it took my wife some time to adjust her packing style. With them being such a short trip away, making a quick weekend visit became very convenient. Despite the brevity of our visit, my wife looked like she was packing for a summer vacation. Notorious for "just in case" clothes, she packs for all occasions. It was funny watching her father raise his brows and question why she packed so heavily. It was his polite way of saying, "Don't get too comfortable." Most of us want our family to feel welcomed, but "make yourself at home" is just a polite gesture, not a challenge.

While I've never struggled packing lightly while traveling, I do at times have this struggle spiritually. Sometimes I place too much emphasis on "success," money, and business. Matthew 6 warns us of placing our affections on earthly things by telling us not to store up for ourselves treasure on earth. No, this passage is not a minimalistic challenge to own less than 5 items. The meaning of this passage is that we should not treasure earthly treasures. More plainly, we should not place our dearest affections on temporary things. For example, it is fine for us to make money; it is not alright when we allow money to make us. I imagine when we get these things out of order our heavenly Father is much like my father-in-law, shaking his head and thinking "Don't get too comfortable."

As a leader, people watch what you do. What direction are you pointing people in? Are you asking others to follow you as you follow Christ, or are you pursuing all this world has to offer? If you want to maintain an eternal perspective while leading in a temporal world, turn your attention toward today's application.

Application

1. Recognize that home is where the heart is: Although cliche, it is true. We are just pilgrims passing through this world. Be careful not to give this world your heart.

2. Make money, but don't love it: Money is not the root of all evil, but the love of it is. Be sure to keep your identity rooted in Christ as you achieve worldly success.

3. Fix your gaze: When you focus on things that are eternal, you will fix your ways. Having a kingdom perspective will keep your heart and behavior pleasing to Christ.

Supplication

Father, keep my affection and heart set on things that matter to you. Help me not to become wrapped up in the temporal, with eyes fixed on eternity. Amen.

Implementation

Reflect on your own life and the things you value most. Are these affections in line with the kingdom of God? If not, what changes can you make to become more Christ-centered in your affections?

_____
_____
_____
_____
_____
_____
_____

Day 26

Attitude

/at-i-tood/
n. a feeling or emotion toward a fact or state

Information

I can do all things through Christ who gives me strength.
—Philippians 4:13 NIV

On your mark, get set, go!" Powering out of my stance like a rocket, I thought there was no way I could lose the race. As a cocky little kid, I surely thought I could do all things. My opponent went from my peripheral view to me staring at her hair blowing in the wind. Struggling to the finish line behind my opponent was a dagger to my pride. I spent the rest of the day crying in the house in disbelief from losing to my mom in a race! I was a sore loser whose ego knew no limitations. I realized that day that "all things" also encompass losing.

I apologize if this devotional is a letdown to your gym wall scripture, but Paul's writings in Philippians 4 are a reference to proper behavior in all circumstances, not achieving record-breaking accomplishments. It has been said that two things define a person—

how they behave with nothing and how they behave with everything. Economic hardships should not send a leader spiraling into depression, and wealth should not prove one arrogant. Paul learned contentment in all situations, as evidenced by the backdrop of his writings, prison.

Could you imagine writing such a masterful lesson on contentment from a prison cell? I pray you never find yourself in that situation, but if Paul can learn contentment under those circumstances, we should be able to live it out in our daily lives. Today's application will reveal the keys to being content in every situation.

Application

1. Don't get too low: Trouble in this world is a promise, but your response is a choice. Don't allow the lows of life cause you to behave below Christ's standard.
2. Don't get too high: Life consists of seasons. As sure as there is summer, there will be winter. Approach abundance with a heart of gratitude, not arrogance.
3. Rely on Christ: Paul was clear on the source of his strength. Accomplishment can only be found through Christ. Apart from him, we can do nothing. It is in Christ that we live, move, and function.

Supplication

With you, I can do all things, and apart from you, I can do nothing. Father, please give me the power to be humble when all is well and stable when circumstances are less than favorable. I'll trust you for strength in all things. Amen.

Implementation

Consider a recent achievement in your life and how you felt during that time. In those moments, how can you keep a Christ-centered attitude about success?

_____

_____

_____

_____

_____

_____

_____

Day 27

Proactive

*/proh-**ak**-tiv/*
adj. acting in anticipation of future problems, needs, or changes

Information

> *Catch for us the foxes, the little foxes that ruin the vineyards, our vineyards that are in bloom.*
>
> —Song of Solomon 2:15 NIV

There's one thing that all of the women in my life hate … pests! My mother will gladly pack her bags and evacuate her home at the sight of a rodent or snake. My wife thinks we should contact pest control experts at the sign of any insect—roaches, ants, spiders, Godzilla…any critter. Normally, her bug sightings are followed by a loud screech commanding me to come and kill whatever it is. On the other hand, I tend to be laid back when it comes to non-life-threatening pests. My attitude matches what I see, their attitudes correspond with what they believe one bug represents. They don't see the baby spider; they see the big momma spider and her 100 babies.

Leaders should match the energy of my wife and mother when dealing with life and organizational pests. Solomon articulates in our focal verse that it is often the small and seemingly innocent things that destroy our most valuable assets. It's the small surface-level issues left unaddressed that overrun our lives.

What have you tolerated in your life that needs to be stepped on? Below are steps to get rid of pesky critters in your life and change what you tolerate.

Application

1. Don't ignore little things: It's the small things in life and leadership that make the biggest difference. Cutting corners today will greatly change the long-term trajectory of your path.
2. Kill it now: Address issues when you notice them, not when you feel like it. Leaving problems unaddressed often paints a picture of acceptance.
3. Be direct: Mistrust is bred from confusion. Others will appreciate your honesty, even if the answer is not what they were hoping for.

Supplication

Father, I humbly ask for your guidance and strength as I strive to be proactive as a leader. Give me wisdom to identity and rectify any issues that pose a threat to myself and those in my care. Amen.

Implementation

What are some things that you have overlooked in the past that may cause bigger issues in the future? How do you plan to address those issues more proactively?

_____

_____

Proactive

Day 28

Patience

*/**pey**-shuhns/*
n. the capacity, habit, or fact of being patient

Information

So Samuel took the horn of oil and anointed him in the presence of his brothers, and from that day on the spirit of the Lord came powerfully upon David.

—1 Samuel 16:13 NIV

But David went back and forth from Saul to tend his father's sheep at Bethlehem.

—1 Samuel 17:15 NIV

Never have I questioned my elementary math teacher more than after reading 1 Samuel 16 and 17. I know I learned that 17 follows 16 numerically, but these two passages just don't make sense. In chapter 16 David was anointed in front of all of his family to be king. Can you guess what followed? If you are like me, you probably predicted a parade, a red carpet, and a police escort to the palace. Nevertheless, the story reveals that David went back to Bethlehem to tend his father's sheep, despite the less glamourous nature of the task. These two passages certainly don't match our modern-day expectation of being crowned king. When we are chosen, we make sure everyone knows it by hash tagging and posting pictures of ourselves on top of the world. It is hard for us to imagine being anointed king but still having to tend to sheep. However, David shows we can be chosen by God for a position and not physically occupy the seat yet.

David exemplified maturity by balancing his vision of where God was leading him with faithfulness to his current position. That is the challenge of a leader and visionary. Can God show you His plans for you tomorrow and still have you faithful today? God is looking for mature leaders to trust in this fast-paced generation we are living in. It is in your patience that God can prepare you for your calling. God used where David was to equip him for where he was headed. We can learn a lot from David about handling great callings. Our application section outlines tips to help us handle great callings with patience.

Application

1. Be patient in the process: You may be next, but you won't get to the next without now.

2. Be faithful in a few: Can you serve before you reign? By David being faithful to the few, he was blessed to rule over many. David went from taking care of sheep to being responsible for a nation.

3. Don't be prideful in promotion: Allowing promotion to make you arrogant is the first sign that God can't trust you with more. God hates a proud spirit. If he sees you can be trusted with more and maintain your character, that is when he can open the floodgates.

Supplication

Father, help me to be patient while you prepare me for my calling. I pray for maturity to balance the vision of tomorrow with the reality of today. Amen.

Implementation

What are some things in your life that have taken longer than you expected to come to fruition? What can you work on while you wait?

_____

_____

_____

_____

_____

_____

_____

Day 29

Adapt

/uh-*dapt*/
v. to make fit often by modification

Information

> *Since they could not get him to Jesus because of the crowd, they made an opening in the roof above Jesus by digging through it and then lowered the mat the man was lying on.*
>
> —Mark 2:4 NIV

Most football players seldom contemplate how wide the field is, but my college coach made sure that the metric 53.3 yards was ingrained in my mind. That number amongst many other things about football is forever etched into my memory. I learned every gap, stunt, coverage, and technique imaginable. While the size, speed, and athleticism of SEC athletes greatly differed from the guys I played against in high school, that was not the biggest adjustment I had to make. I was handed a playbook on my first day on campus that rivaled my physics, calculus, and chemistry books. In college, football players are not freestyling; it is a game of strategy. We had plans for our plans and were ready at any moment to adjust or change our play based on the alignment of our opponents. The play started well before the ball was snapped as we played mental games with the opposing team.

We see a similar scenario laying out in Mark chapter 2 when the friends of the paralyzed man called a play that had worked so many times for others. So many times in the past, people had walked up to Jesus and received healing, and these guys planned to do the same. However, Jesus' popularity presented a problem for them. They could not make their way to Jesus via traditional methods. Stuck at the door, they decided to tear the roof off to get to Jesus. Talk about a plan B! Mike Tyson once said, "Everyone has a plan until they get punched in the face." Well, they had a plan for a punch. Failure was not an option! They adjusted their plans, got their hands dirty, and displayed massive faith.

Just because things don't go exactly according to your plan on paper doesn't mean you should give up. As leaders, it is important to recognize that our methodologies may change as we seek to accomplish our mission. Embedded in this text is a wealth of wisdom we can apply to our lives when plans do not go as anticipated.

Application

1. Adapt: When plan A doesn't work, you must adapt. Like a quarterback changing the play at the line of scrimmage based on the defense's alignment, you must be willing to adjust the play call to advance the mission.

2. Embrace: There are those who thrive in uncertainty and others who shrink. As leaders, you can't be afraid of change and hard work. One thing in life is certain—uncertainty.

3. Believe: The four friends lowered their paralyzed brother in faith that he would walk out of that house as it would have been much more difficult to raise a paralyzed man back up by working against gravity. Having faith that your organization will accomplish its mission

is what will inspire you to seek alternative paths and make bold moves.

Supplication

When my plans don't work, God, please help me to trust and believe that there is another way. I pray for wisdom to discern alternatives and for a spirit of perseverance to endure. Amen.

Implementation

What are some areas in your life where your plans have not gone as scripted, but you still wish to achieve the intended outcome? What changes can you make to still accomplish the mission?

_____

_____

_____

_____

_____

_____

_____

Day 30

Purpose

*/**pur**-puhs/*
n. something set up as an end to be attained: intention

Information

Therefore, since we are surrounded by such a great cloud of witnesses, let us throw off everything that hinders and the sin that so easily entangles. And let us run with perseverance the race marked out for us, fixing our eyes on Jesus, the pioneer, and perfecter of faith. For the joy set before him, he endured the cross, scorning its shame, and sat down at the right hand of the throne of God. Consider him who endured such opposition from sinners, so that you will not grow weary and lose heart.

—Hebrews 12:1-3 NIV

"Alex, can you tell us why you play the game with such passion?" This was a question I was asked by a reporter during my time playing football at Texas A&M. My response was this: "I play for the name on my chest, the name on my back, and the name on my heart." For those of you unfamiliar with the layout of my football jersey—the name on my chest was Texas A&M, which represents my community. The name on my back was Sezer, which represents family. Last, and most important, the name on my heart is Jesus Christ, my God and salvation.

This, my friend, is a critical facet of success in life and leadership—operating for something bigger than you. Those who transcend boundaries and break barriers go beyond the technicalities and intellectual understanding of what they do; they tap into the purpose for which they work. They go beyond going through the motions and operate on a mission. Now, before you ascribe credit to me for this ideal, please note, this is Jesus' model.

In Hebrews 12, the writer encourages Christians to persevere and endure in this world, while upholding their faith. Thankfully, he didn't just give a command, but a guide on how we should do this. He pointed to the model of Christ who used his purpose to produce perseverance. Jesus endured the cross "for the joy set before him." The purpose of his suffering produced perseverance during his suffering. Likewise, if we aim to be people of perseverance, we should follow his model. Let's go deeper.

Application

1. Drop the weight: One key to living on purpose is to clear the table of the things that distract from that purpose. Paul illustrated the importance of this by commanding Christians to lay aside the weight and sin which hinders us.

2. Look to Jesus: We have a model and a mentor in Christ. If you aim to be a purpose-driven person, you should fix your eyes on Jesus and his teachings.

3. Consider the joy: As one writer said, "Compete to obtain the prize." It is so easy to get bogged down by the things we must endure and forget why we do what we do. Remember your organization's objectives—whether it be wealth or community impact.

Supplication

Father, help me to consider the joy set before me as I endure as a Christian in this world. Help me never to pursue gain with selfish motives, and keep my eyes locked on you. Amen.

Implementation

Take some time to consider the joy set before you as a Christian leader. What are you excited about in the future that gives you motivation for today?

_____
_____
_____
_____
_____
_____
_____

Made in the USA
Middletown, DE
20 July 2023

34914013R00078